The Wine of Cana

The Wine of Cana

Fr. Ludger Grün, SSPX

2915 Forest Avenue | Kansas City, MO 64109

©2015 by Fr. Ludger Grün, SSPX
All rights reserved.

Originally published by STAS Editions.

ANGELUS PRESS
2915 Forest Avenue
Kansas City, Missouri 64109
Phone (816) 753-3150
Fax (816) 753-3557
Order Line 1-800-966-7337
www.angeluspress.org

ISBN 978-1-937843-87-8
FIRST PRINTING—May 2015

Printed in the United States of America

Marriage is
a daily
work
of the heart

Table of Contents

Foreword	3
The Wedding of Cana	5
The Plan and Counsel of God	11
The Sacrament of Matrimony	15
The Effect of the Sacrament of Matrimony	16
The Helping Graces of the Sacrament of Matrimony	18
The Divine Bride and Groom	21
Jesus Christ, the Bridegroom of the Church	24
Love of Christ for His Bride during His Life	24
Love of Christ for His Bride in His Passion and Cross	26
Love of Christ for His Bride in His Resurrection, Ascension and the Descent of the Holy Ghost	27
Love of Christ for His Bride in His Ministry	28
The Catholic Church, the Bride of Jesus Christ	31
The Head and the Body	35
The Common Life of Christ and the Church	38
Life for their Children	42
Living out the Sacrament of Matrimony	46
Signs of Love	48
Forgiving is Living	51
Order and Structure	53
The Children	55
The Parents as the Image and Likeness of the Creator	59
The Parents as an Image of Christ and the Church	62
Downwards or Upwards?	66

Foreword

This is not a book of "one-thousand tips for a happy marriage." There are many books that one can find with many suggestions and valuable pieces of advice,[1] but most of them lack a truly Christian basis and they do not treat marriage as a sacrament.

This book would like to invite its reader on a journey. On this path we will look at the beginning of the world, focus on the end and completion of creation as well as its central theme, and what part the Christian married couple plays in it. All this will serve the true understanding of marriage as a sacrament.

Like a traveler, we want to study the map before we start walking. A traveler has to make this journey on his own, one step at a time, in order for him to keep moving forward and reach his destination. It would be childish to think that one can reach the top of a mountain with one step, or that by just by reading the roadmap one can reach his destination. With this said, it would be fatal to ask of this book to give some kind of ideal recipe to attain every goal today and now. This would just lead to being overwhelmed, discouraged and self-righteous.

What was the characteristic mistake of the Pharisees? They wanted to look good in front of the people, without acknowledging their own weaknesses and faults. Their fault was hypocrisy; taken literally it is putting on an act.

---

[1] E.g. "The 5 Love Languages" by Gary D. Chapman.

Thus, one would immediately become an archenemy of Christ, if one simply wanted to play the "role of Christ and the Church" in marriage without looking at the same time at one's own weakness and misery. In the delicate and sometimes difficult situation where two people live together, it can be quite destructive and grueling when one or both partners stick with a "role" and hide behind it. Readers beware! The role in question is not a part in a play but a fact of life. To these facts belong one's position as member of Christ and the Church and also the reality of one's own personality.

This includes one's own character, temperament, talents and abilities as well as one's faults, weaknesses and limitations. If we do not pay attention to these points, it will result in artificializing and distorting the relationship of the couple and all the grave consequences this entails.

This book is also not meant to give one partner the power to tell the other how he is supposed to act. Here too this applies:

He that is without sin among you, let him first cast a stone at her! [2]

It is rather intended as a great encouragement for the married couple, when they see how Jesus and Mary come to their aid, what great connection their marriage bears and what wonderful chances their marriage gives them to live in the Kingdom of God. This book should also be a reminder that marriage is appointed for the glorification of God throughout life; in the sacrament of marriage the spouses pray, "Hallowed be Thy Name, Thy Kingdom come." If they try to follow this precept, then these words of Christ apply:

For where there are two or three gathered together in my name, there am I in the midst of them. [3]

---

[2] Jn 8,7
[3] Mt 18,20

The Wedding of Cana

And the third day, there was a marriage in Cana of Galilee: and the mother of Jesus was there. And Jesus was also invited, and his disciples, to the marriage. And the wine failing, the mother of Jesus saith to him: 'They have no wine.' And Jesus saith to her: 'Woman, what is that to me and to thee? My hour is not yet come.' His mother saith to the waiters: 'Whatsoever he shall say to you, do ye.' Now there were set there six water pots of stone, according to the manner of the purifying of the Jews, containing two or three measures apiece. Jesus saith to them: 'Fill the water pots with water.' And they filled them up to the brim. And Jesus saith to them: 'Draw out now, and carry to the chief steward of the feast.' And they carried it. And when the chief steward had tasted the water made wine, and knew not whence it was, but the waiters knew who had drawn the water; the chief steward calleth the bridegroom, and saith to him: 'Every man at first setteth forth good wine, and when men have well drunk, then that which is worse. But thou hast kept the good wine until now.' This beginning of miracles did Jesus in Cana of Galilee; manifested his glory, and his disciples believed in him. [4]

In this wedding, we can distinguish and identify three stages.

The first stage is characterized by the wine, which the bride and the groom have prepared. It would be improper to celebrate a wedding feast with only mineral water.

Wine gladdens the heart of man. [5]

---

[4] Jn 2,1
[5] Ps 104,15

This wine is an expression of festive joy, the happiness of the newlyweds that they have found each other and now can begin the new chapter of their married life. It is an expression of sheer willpower of the married couple: "You will always be someone special to me!" It is an expression of love from the word of the Canticle of Canticles:

Your love is more precious than wine! [6]

Therefore, what we can see in this wine is a symbol of first love.

Is it not a hidden worry for the married couple to see this first love die sooner than they imagined? The celebration goes on, the guests are happy and everybody is filled with hope that this marriage would be a happy one. This expectation can be seen strongly on the faces of the newlyweds, as they are looking around with pride and amazement that this wedding feast is taking place for them. Wine is for them an expression of joy and love!

Then comes the second stage: Before long, the first wine is running out. It is almost ironic; what is happening in this wedding happens in some cases much later: The first love seems to disappear and is replaced by everyday life.

Only water remains! Whether this first love is only obscured or totally gone, the fact is, one has ended up in simple everyday life sooner than expected. Water is a daily drink, necessary and vital, but nevertheless bland and transparent. Imagine the disappointment on their faces, the feeling of having been deceived! What about all the declarations of love and future hopes? What about the "You will always be special to me!" Water is important; it is essential, but in marriage, one looks for more than that. The groom is losing face; the bride asks him, "Is that all you can offer?"

Where should we go from here? Should we be realistic? Should we turn to the principles of the world: "You can't get anything for free!" The bride and the groom are already con-

---

[6] Cant. 1,2

sidering how to deal with this embarrassment. Should they go on quietly serving the guests with water, pretending that everything is just fine? Indeed, many married couples practice this attitude: "But this is normal!" Later we will see that this is not at all that evident in the eyes of God.

This is a stage that is well known by the "world". From this comes pessimism, which keeps many relationships from becoming a marriage. Many young people do not get married anymore and live against God's commandments. They live together because they have lost confidence that a marriage can be durable. [7]

That also explains the frequent changing of partners. When the stage of everyday life sets in, worldly thinking people have no idea how to believe in a continuing, ever-growing love. Then it comes to where young people have new acquaintances every three to six months and old acquaintances turn into "exes." Some could even show off with a "collection of exes". In between they go out with their "ex" from last year because "we are still good friends." Many "remarried" divorcees speak of the same problem.

Generally, the works of Eric Kästner are not to be recommended. However, in one poem he was able to describe very well the disappointment of first love:

Objective Romance

> After knowing each other for eight long years
> (and one could say they knew each other well),
> his love was lost, and so was hers
> like people lose their hat or coat.
>
> The two felt sad, tried to act happy, kissed,
> pretending everything is okay.
> They looked at each other, feeling bad.
> she finally cries, and he stands by, helpless.
>
> From the window you can see a ship setting sail.

---

[7] Consider the jokes about marriage. Most have a pessimistic view of marriage.

> he said it was a quarter past four.
> Time for coffee, somewhere.
> Someone was playing the piano next door.
>
> They went to the smallest cafe in town
> and silently stirred in their cups.
> In the evening, they still sat there.
> They sat alone, didn't speak a word,
> Couldn't grasp what had happened.

It is not always that drastic. In most cases, love has somehow fallen asleep and is covered up by a routine. If a serious illness or an accident occurs, suddenly a deep connection appears! Then the crying and worrying at the bedside will not end!

The third stage: Mary, the mother of Jesus, was there. With her gentle, all-seeing love, she notices the distress of the newlyweds. She does not go to them saying, "My children, such is life. You are getting nothing for free. You must face that life is cold, hard and empty of joy. And do not expect anything from a marriage!" No! Mary knew that the hearts of men were created to love and to be loved! So had the Creator made men in the beginning, to live for Love!

It is not good for man to be alone![8]

Mary goes to Jesus to tell Him of the misery of the bride and groom. Jesus does not reject her but reminds her that His hour has not yet come. With His hour, He means His work of salvation through the cross, where from His pierced Heart, His Bride, the Church, is born! It is not yet time for His own wedding to come, even though He, the Bridegroom is already present[9] and wants to serve His own wedding wine! He commanded them to fill six stone jars with water up to the brim. Then he let the servants bring the stone jars to the chief steward. This headwaiter was a wine expert but he could not determine where the wine was from. *"Mosel? Chianti? Chilean? Californian Zinfandel? Bordeaux?"* he must have asked himself... It was indeed a wine that comes from a heavenly wedding. Every jar contained two

---

[8] Gen 2,18
[9] Mt 9,15

to three measures, a measure equaled approximately 10 gallons. That makes about 150 gallons of wine!

One must admit, it is indeed a striking miracle. One could easily understand when Jesus healed the blind to see or the lame were able to walk. But to donate 150 gallons of wine! Imagine a truck with 800 bottles of the best wine to be delivered free to a wedding reception! You would never forget that! Yet Jesus did not exaggerate; that is not His style. Not only was the amount amazing but also the quality of the wine! The headwaiter then calls the groom and points out to him that the new wine was much better than the first wine!

Therefore, this wine is served to the newlyweds and the guests. Faces are glowing again, the disappointment is forgotten. Once again, the wedding feast continues with joy and relief. The supply of wine gives the young couple the confidence that with the blessing of Jesus, love will never die! What a love! The first wine represents first love. The new wine that Jesus gives is better than the first. Here lies the great promise of Jesus, that He would implant into the hearts of the spouses a love that is more beautiful, more serious and more solid than the first love!

The love of God is poured forth in our hearts![10]

Later, we will see what the sacrament of marriage means for the spouses. Here we just want to state that a Christian marriage has much greater riches than worldly marriage. The world does not know the third stage of marriage! They only know the first and the second stage and live with this conviction: "You can't get anything for free in this world!" We can even find it in psalms:

Many say, Who shows us good things?[11]

The many divorcees and concubines of today, as well as "remarried" people share in this pessimism. They do not expect anything anymore once the first love has died. However, Mary wanted to save the bride and the groom from Cana and

---

[10] Rom 5,5
[11] Ps 4,6

all married couples from that disappointment. She believed in the love of Jesus and His power to pour that new and wonderful love in the hearts of all men.

The question is: Do we believe in this love of Jesus? Or are we contaminated with that pessimism of the world looking at marriage with doubting eyes? Is it perhaps that this idea is also hidden in our hearts: that marriage is a gamble? Here is a question to be asked: Do we see marriage with the eyes of God or with the eyes of the world?

The Plan and Counsel of God

In order for us to see the beauty and greatness of a Christian marriage, we have to step back and look at the plan that God has had from the start. Then, we will realize that a Christian marriage is like a flowering twig, wholly and greatly intertwined on a mighty tree.

St. Thomas Aquinas has spoken of the goals in general: *The goal comes first according to the intention, but last as to the execution.*[12] When someone wants to drive to New Orleans, he must first have the intention to go there. The destination itself is only reached in the end.

One can ask: What was God's intention with the creation? What is the whole purpose of the history of humankind? What is with these vicissitudes of the centuries? What is the goal of divine providence from day to day? Why does God allow so much evil in this world? Why does he permit such suffering? Where does the wind of the Holy Ghost blow, he that is working in our hearts? If we want our many questions to be answered, we have to look at the end, where everything evolves! A glance at the end and at the peak of the history of humanity makes us understand what God has planned from the start. In the last book of the Holy Scripture, the Apocalypse of St. John, we will find the answer to our questions:

> *And I saw a new heaven and a new earth. For the first heaven and the first earth passed away, and the sea is no more. And I saw the holy city, the New Jerusalem, coming down out of heaven from God, made ready as a bride adorned for her husband. (...)*

---

[12] "Super Sent." lib. 4 d. 14 q. 1 a. 2

That is so important that St. John had to say it again:

And there came one of the seven angels who had the vials full of the seven last plagues; and spoke with me: 'Come, I will show thee the bride, the spouse of the Lamb.' And he took me up in spirit to a great and high mountain, and he showed me the holy city Jerusalem, coming down out of heaven from God, having the glory of God, and the light thereof was like to a precious stone, as to the jasper stone, even as crystal.[13]

At the end of mankind's history, we will find at its zenith the Church as the bride and the spouse of Christ, adorned with glory for Him! *The bride and spouse of the Lamb* – It all comes down to this! The Church as the bride and temple of God!

The same is said by St. Paul in his epistle to the Ephesians describing the counsel of God:

And this His good pleasure He purposed in Him to be dispensed in the fullness of the times; to re-establish all things in Christ, both those in the heavens and those on the earth.[14]

In Greek "re-establish" literally means "to put under a head." Christ as head of his Mystical Body! His Mystical Body is but the Church: *He is the Head of the Body, the Church.*[15] Head and body are also taken by St. Paul to describe the relationship between husband and wife in marriage.

A husband is head of the wife, just as Christ is head of the Church, being Himself savior of the body.[16]

That is the meaning and fulfillment of the whole history of humanity: Christ, the Lamb of God with His bride, the Church.[17]

The kingdom of heaven is like a king who held a wedding feast for his son.[18]

---

[13] Apoc. 21,9 ff.
[14] Eph 1,9
[15] Col 1,18
[16] Eph 5,23
[17] Of course, the Church is the Roman Catholic Church as Pope Pius XII points out in his Encyclical *Mystici Corporis*, 29.6.1943
[18] Mt 22,2

With these words of the Gospel, one may think the comparison is accidental. But in fact, it is all about the main plan of the kingdom of God! We already know the passage:

And he said to me, 'Write: Blessed are those who are called to the marriage supper of the Lamb.' [19]

Other words of the Gospel remind us of the wedding of the Lamb of God:

Then will the kingdom of heaven be like ten virgins who took their lamps and went forth to meet the bridegroom and the bride. Five of them were foolish and five wise. But the five foolish, when they took their lamps, took no oil with them, while the wise did take oil in their vessels with the lamps. Then as the bridegroom was long in coming, they all become drowsy and slept. And at midnight a cry arose, 'Behold, the bridegroom is coming, go forth to meet him!" [20]

We can find a connection between this Gospel and the Epistle of St. Paul to the Ephesians, which speaks of the intentions of Christ:

Husbands, love your wives, just as Christ loved the Church, and delivered himself up for her, that he might sanctify her (...) in order that he might present to himself the Church in all her glory, not having spot or wrinkle or any such thing, but that she might be holy and without blemish. [21]

This shows the deep meaning of Christian marriage: It is closely linked to the central topic of human history and the great plans of God for humanity. For in the sacrament of matrimony, spouses are involved in this plan and live it, together with Christ and the Church.

Because of this close connection between Christian marriage and the history of salvation St. Paul highly values the sacrament of matrimony whenever he speaks of it:

---

[19] Apoc. 19,9
[20] Mt 25,1
[21] Eph 5,25

This is a great mystery — I mean in reference to Christ and to the Church.[22]

St. Paul calls marriage a mystery. When do we speak of a mystery in faith? The mystery of Incarnation, the mystery of the Holy Trinity, the mystery of the Divine Presence of Christ in the Holy Sacrament,...Every time faith looks at something that is too great for the human mind to comprehend, we call it a mystery. It simply extends far beyond human intellect and seems dark to the observer. So, when St. Paul calls the sacrament of matrimony a mystery, he wants the spouses to realize the greatness of their vocation: That in which they live every day is so profound and important that the human intellect cannot help but be left in amazement!

How much does the superficial, everyday thinking that does not want to see anything special in it, ignore reality! St. Paul indeed is far from this idea, that marriage, over time, only represents something reduced, something unhappy, that disappoints the initial hopes in the beginning!

Furthermore, we will first look at the effects of the sacrament of marriage. This will show us the place the spouses take in the great plan of God.

After that, we will turn to the origin and the root of Christian marriage – Christ and the Church – and describe the love that connects both. Christian marriage should take the love out of this connection.

---

[22] Eph 5,32

The Sacrament of Matrimony

To many the Sacrament of Matrimony is the icing on the cake: here are two who love each other, and now God also agrees for them to be together! To others, marriage is a sacrament only because it occasionally means great difficulties. So a special help is needed to be able to overcome these! But by that, we again arrive at the "worldly" perception of marriage, which shows a deep sense of pessimism! The Sacrament of Matrimony is much more! First, let us look at the other sacraments:

By the Church's teaching, we know the effects of the sacraments. We know that in Baptism, original sin is forgiven and we become children of God. The child is not "a little bit" baptized, it really is a child of God. In Holy Communion, we receive the Body of Our Lord Jesus Christ. Here it also applies: We do not receive Jesus "a little bit" but truly, substantially and really! In Confession, we obtain the forgiveness of our sins. It is not a weak sign but actual forgiveness.

Every sacrament gives an assured effect. When someone is being ordained as a priest, he is not considered somewhat a priest after the ordination, but he is simply a priest. In Confirmation, one receives the Holy Ghost and has a distinct mark on his soul that can never be erased. Each sacrament is established by Christ as a holy symbol that brings forth certainly and clearly the grace as indicated in the sign.

So now, we are faced with the question: What is the effect of the Sacrament of Matrimony?

The Effect of the Sacrament of Matrimony

In the sacrament of Matrimony, the Christian marriage forms a continuation, an expansion of the marriage of Christ and the Church. Two baptized individuals are bound together in matrimony. Through baptism, they are already members of the Mystical Body of Christ; they are in Christ and in the Church.[23] At their wedding, their union becomes through the sacrament a budding branch attached to the bond of Christ and the Church.[24] Jesus said, *"I am the vine, you are the branches."*[25] These words have special meaning for married spouses. Their union stands in a living and not merely symbolic union with the heavenly bridal couple, Christ and the Church. Just as it is unimaginable to have a branch without the tree, without the focus on Christ, it is not possible to understand what connects the newlyweds on their wedding day. This does not only come from their baptism but rather particularly from the sacrament of matrimony.

Bishop Fulton Sheen wrote, *Most lives are like doors without hinges or sleeves without coats, or bows without violins; that is, unrelated to wholes or purposes which give them meaning.*[26] The marriage of Christians can be understood only when one understands the fact that the marriage is a whole with the union of Christ and the Church.

Let us stay with this picture for a little while: If a winegrower works on the twigs of a vine, he trims or binds them high. Does he do that only to the branches or still more to the vine itself? When there is a rustling wind blowing through the branches, does it not also affect the tree itself? On the other hand, when a bird sits on a tree, does it not sit on a branch, too? If someone breaks a branch, does he not also hurt the tree?

---

[23] Unless they are separated from the Bride of Christ by heresy or schism.
[24] The famous theologian Scheeben says: *The best way to describe the position of Christian marriage in the union of Christ and the Church is to say that it is a branching or spin-off of this union.*
[25] Jn 15,5
[26] F. Sheen, "The seven virtues."

The same goes for our body: When a doctor treats a wound, he helps the patient and not just his wounded hand. If we look someone in the eye, we look at the person as a whole. In all this it is clear: What happens to the part happens to the whole.

From this we can see the dignity of Christian marriage: Christian spouses are taking part in the dignity of Christ and the Church. Indeed, they are a part of the great mystery that exists through the whole history of humanity; they are directly connected to the great plan of God and grafted into it.

We want to emphasize here that Christian marriage is not just a symbol or an image of the eternal bride and groom. Beyond this image, we find between the Christian spouses and the eternal bridal couple a supernatural connection of life, just like between the branch and the tree!

The husband is the representative of Christ, the wife the representative of the Church. What the husband does to his wife, he does it to the whole Church, whom Christ loves so much. And what the wife does to her husband, she does it to Christ himself. So St. Paul directly said:

Let wives be subject to their husbands as to the Lord. [27]

What significance does the love in a marriage have! Every loving word, every gesture, every attentiveness has a great value! Indeed, one can say that the love in marriage amounts to the love spouses have for God. One cannot genuflect in front of the tabernacle and then be cold and repulsive at home! It is not surprising if we think of the words of Jesus:

As long as you did it for one of these, the least of my brethren, you did it for me! [28]

These words reach a special significance and fulfilment in marriage.

This connection with the bridal couple, Christ and the Church, has also another encouraging side: A married couple is never alone; it is carried and safe in God's love. The branch does

---

[27] Eph 5,22
[28] Mt 25,40

not have to bear fruits alone; it can rely constantly on the trunk to which it is attached. Is that not the reason why Jesus donated so much wine to the couple at Cana; because they should love each other, not with their own strength, but with God's love? That portends a great calmness and a profound trust!

Helping Graces of the Sacrament of Matrimony

Jesus is always there, helping the spouses with His graces. However, what do these graces want? This can be shown easily in an example: Imagine a winegrower going through his vineyard looking at the ripening fruits. He goes from one grapevine to another; grapes are growing everywhere. But he would certainly be surprised if on a branch, instead of grapes he found bananas...

That is perhaps a strange example, but it is purposely chosen. Because a married couple is that disordered if it does not resemble Christ and the Church in its daily life. With that, the answer to our question is given: The graces of the sacrament of matrimony help the spouses to be like the heavenly bride and groom, Christ and the Church. The branch should match the tree! The more one is faithful to God's graces, the more noticeable Christ and the Church are in the lives of the spouses. Cardinal Billot said, in a treatise on the sacrament of marriage, that the helping graces are "conforming" the spouses to Christ and the Church.

Through grace, spouses are adapted – also spiritually – to the mystery of Christ and the Church.[29]

This adaptation only makes sense when they put it into practice. We will hear more about it further below.

Christ expects suitable fruits from the branches of His vines:

I am the true vine, and my Father is the vinedresser. Every branch in me that bears no fruit, he will take away; and every

---

[29] Card. Billot, "De Eccl. Sacramentis," 7.Ed. Vol II, p. 355.

branch that bears fruit he will cleanse, that it may bear more fruit. [30]

That also applies to marriage. How many Christian marriages set that completely aside! With good intention and often with great efforts they practice the faith, but it does not occur to them, to make their marriage similar to that of the heavenly bride and groom, Christ and the Church! This is a field that has not been ploughed. It is also seen in the way some married people go to confession. They confess that they were impatient or lenient in bringing up their children. However, much less often, they confess things like, "I didn't give time to my wife, I instead sit long hours in front of the computer. I did not really pay attention to what she was saying. I was cold and indifferent to her. I did not give her what she needed the most. I have made our life together dull..."

Many resemble the man with the talent that is written in the gospel: Instead of using the opportunity to put his talent to use, he had just buried it. When his master came back from his trip, he gave back exactly the same talent. He was then severely punished because he did not use the talent that his master had given him!

Some married couples have settled for a lifestyle where there is minimal tension. They live together, often side by side depending on the inclinations, emotions, moods and the necessities of one's daily needs. Of course, there are also nice moments, but what difference is there between this couple and the "worldly" couple? Should we not say that they are more or less just living moment to moment? There is a passage in the gospel that leaves one pretty perplexed:

And the next day, after they had left Bethany, he felt hungry. And seeing in the distance a fig tree in leaf, he went to see if he might find anything on it. But when he came up to it, he found nothing but leaves; for it was not the season for figs. Then he spoke to it saying, 'May no one ever eat fruit of thee henceforward forever.' And his disciples heard. And as they passed by in

---

[30] Jn 15,1f

the morning, they saw the fig tree withered from the roots. And Peter remembering, said to him, 'Rabbi, behold, the fig tree that thou didst curse is withered up.' [31]

"In fact, it was not yet season for figs." Christ searched for fig fruits on the tree, although by nature none could be expected! At first glance, it is very strange. One is perhaps tempted to think it is unjust. Jesus expected fruits from that tree beyond the natural order. At that time (out of season), the tree could not bear fruit. It lived the way a fig tree does: roots in the soil, green leaves and twigs in the wind, birds in the tree, everything as usual! Jesus, however, gives men supernatural gifts which can bear supernatural fruits. The puzzle is solved: This fig tree is a picture of men; Jesus came to them with His graces but they just continued live as if nothing had happened.

He came unto his own, and his own received him not! [32]

The fig tree and the man with the single talent have something in common: their course of life was not changed, even though Our Lord has come into their lives. What would we say if in the gospel from Cana they reported, *However, the newlyweds went and stored the wine in the cellar and did not touch it for the next 20 years.*? How stern and demanding Jesus is, when it comes to the fruits that we should produce with His grace!

The graces of the sacrament enable us to live assimilated to the wedded couple, Christ and Church. They permit our Lord to find similarities in the life of the couple:

- Similarity of love,
- Similarity of the order of head and body,
- Similarity in the care for the children of God.

This triple fruit will be described later on. First, we have to understand this divine marriage, through faith, because we can only imitate what we know. Looking at Christ and His Church with the eye of faith shows the way that we have to take.

---

[31] Mk 11,12-21
[32] Jn 1,11

The Divine Bride and Groom

It is obvious that we have to remind ourselves how Christ and the Church represent a nuptial couple.

Jesus loves all men; he died for them. He loves them so as to unite them to His bride – His Church. All the saving, forgiving and holy love of Jesus has as its purpose to unite his brothers and sisters to his Church.

I lay down my life for my sheep. And other sheep I have that are not of this fold. Them also I must bring, and they shall hear my voice, and there shall be one fold and one shepherd. [33]

A whole book of the Old Testament describes the love of the Divine Bride and Groom, Christ and the Church, Solomon's Canticle of Canticles. We can find a classical description of it from St. Bernard of Clairvaux. He reveals how wonderful and pure the love that reigns between the Savior and His Church is. Immature hearts may misinterpret the Canticle of Canticles. Nevertheless, the interpretations of St. Bernard guide us to understand it better.

Behold thou art fair, O my beloved, behold thou art fair, thy eyes are those of doves. (Cant. 1,14) As the lily among thorns, so is my love among the daughters. (Cant. 2,2) Behold, my beloved speaketh to me: Arise, make haste, my love, my dove, my beautiful one, and come. For winter is now past, the rain is over and gone. The flowers have appeared in our land, the time of pruning is come. The voice of turtle is heard in our land. The fig tree hath put forth her green figs. The vines in flower yield their sweet smell. Arise, my love, my beautiful one, and come. My dove in the clefts of the rock, in the hollow place of the wall, show me thy

---

[33] Jn 10,15f

face, let thy voice sound in my ears, for thy voice is sweet, and thy face comely. [34]

Thou hast wounded my heart, my sister, my spouse, thou hast wounded my heart with one of thy eyes, and with one hair of thy neck. How beautiful are thy breasts, my sister, my spouse! Thy love is more beautiful than wine, and the sweet smell of thy ointments above all aromatical spices. Thy lips, my spouse, are as a dropping honeycomb, honey and milk are under my tongue; and the smell of thy garments, as the smell of frankincense. My sister, my spouse, is a garden enclosed, a fountain sealed up. Thy plants are a paradise of pomegranates with the fruits of orchard, cypress with spikenard. [35]

These words from Solomon's Canticle of Canticles are inspired by the Holy Ghost and describe the love that the Groom, Jesus Christ, has for His Bride, the Church. He is delighted by her beauty. She possesses divine beauty by grace that exceeds everything worldly. The splendor of this beauty is also described in the 12th Chapter of the Apocalypse of St. John, wherein the Church is presented as the Woman clothed with the sun. As our eyes cannot tolerate to stare very long into the sun, so it would be overwhelming if we could see the beauty of the Church in its brilliance! However, in the state of grace, every Christian wife possesses this kind of beauty, because through the sacrament she has a mystical participation in the dignity of the Church.

At this point we should add a comment to the whole of Solomon's Canticle of Canticles for this book of the Old Testament describes the love between the heavenly Groom and His Church. Since this is not possible here, we are content with the individual passages.

Behold, thou art fair, O my beloved, thy eyes are those of doves... Thou hast wounded my heart, my sister, my spouse, thou hast wounded my heart with one of thy eyes.

---

[34] Cant. 2,10-14
[35] Cant. 4,9-13

What is it "to be in love"? It is the imprint of love. Someone who is in love cannot imagine a life without his love. It has captured his inner being and, so stricken by love, he cannot, and will not, live without it. Do not we find this state in the Sacred Heart of Jesus? It is wounded because of His love for us and this wound is always present, even after His Resurrection.[36]

Thou hast wounded my heart, my sister, my spouse!

Jesus never wants to be without His Church again, that is why He will lead His bride, the Church, to her eternal home.

Can a woman forget her infant? Does she not have mercy for the fruit of her womb? And if she should forget, yet will not I forget thee! Behold, I have graven thee in my hands: thy walls are always before my eyes. [37]

He has engraved his faithfulness to his bride in his hands, and how much so![38]

What are the eyes of the Church, whose glance ravishes the Sacred Heart of Jesus so much? Is it not the faith of the Church which looks with full simplicity and love towards him? *Be simple as doves!*[39] Because of this faithful look, he responds to all her requests and favors:

Therefore I say to you, all things whatever you ask for in prayer, believe that you shall receive, and they shall come to you. [40]

How wonderful is your love, my sister, my spouse, much sweeter than wine. The Church is wholly and totally fulfilling the new commandment of Jesus.

This is my commandment, that you love one another as I have loved you. [41]

---

[36] Jn 19,34
[37] Is 49,15f
[38] How profoundly wrong are those Christians, who want to make up a Christianity without his Church!
[39] Mt 10,16
[40] Mk 11,24
[41] Jn 15,12

This divine love goes beyond human love. Indeed, as God stands above His creation, so the love of the Church stands above all worldly love. No wonder that Jesus, as a groom, is so very much enraptured by it! The reader should well consider the greatness of this love because it can be found again in the sacrament of matrimony!

> *Arise, make haste, my love, my dove, my beautiful one, and come. For winter is now past, the rain is over and gone. The flowers have appeared in our land, the time of pruning is come. The voice of turtle is heard in our land. The fig tree hath put forth her green figs. The vines in flower yield their sweet smell. Arise, my love, my beautiful one, and come!*

Jesus calls His Bride to be with Him eternally in heaven. The winter season of the Old Testament has passed, the shower of graces has sprinkled the earth and it bears its first fruits.

Jesus Christ, the Bridegroom of the Church

Love of Christ for His Bride during His Life

His whole life, His love was dedicated to His Father and His Bride. It begins on Christmas: Out of love for her, He has taken the form of the flesh through the Incarnation and conformed Himself to this state. He has traversed the infinite distance between Creator and creature just to be like them.

> *The voice of my beloved, behold, he cometh leaping upon the mountains, skipping over the hills. My beloved is like a roe, or a young hart.* [42]

St. Bernard of Clairvaux sees in this verse the Incarnation of Our Lord Jesus Christ. How great the adjustment and compliance must the Groom have undergone in the Incarnation. His poverty and humility in Bethlehem recall the same love. He has done everything just to be like His Bride.

How did He spend the years in Nazareth? They were years of prayer, of work, of sacrifice for His Bride. Other husbands

---

[42] Cant, 2,8f

planned first of having a profession or building a business, but Jesus on the other hand, directed all His actions towards His Bride. She was always the primary factor in His life. These were 30 years of pre-planned loving and consideration.

Even before his public life, he spent 40 days in the desert to fast and pray for her. It was the same before building the foundation of his Church, the summoning of the apostles; he spent that night in prayer for her. The husband may not be the savior of his wife, but why should he not heartily pray for her?

How tenderly has He taken her burden again and again:

And when Jesus had come into Peter's house, he saw Peter's mother-in-law lying in bed, sick with a fever. And he touched her hand, and the fever left her; and she rose and began to wait on them. Now when it was evening, they brought to him many who were possessed, and he cast out the spirits with a word, and cured all who were sick; that what was spoken through Isaias the prophet might be fulfilled, who said, he himself took up our infirmities, and bore the burden of our ills. [43]

Hence, the healing miracles of Jesus were not magic tricks but indeed a work of his love to his brothers and sisters whose burdens he took. Therein, we find a love full of compassion and attachment.

We could continue with a commentary on the whole life of Jesus, but this would burst the seams of this book. This was subtly mentioned by St. John, the beloved disciple:

There are, however, many other things that Jesus did; but if every one of these should be written, not even the world itself, I think, could hold the books that would have to be written. [44]

Everything that Jesus has done, has been done out of His love for His Father and for His Church!

---

[43] Mt 8,14ff
[44] Jn 21,25

Love of Christ for His Bride during His Passion

His love shows especially in His suffering. That is why we want to talk about it here. One single prayer of Jesus was so precious that it would have been enough to save the world. However, why did He choose to suffer that much? The answer most likely is: One single prayer would have been enough for salvation, but not enough to show His burning love for us! It is amazing how far Jesus has gone! The agony in the garden and the sweating of blood, Judas' betrayal, the denial of Peter, were these things not enough already, that He took on himself? However, He still went much further! Scourging, crowning with thorns, death on the cross! His whole body is full of marks of His unending love! But He does not stop there! He has carried the burden of the cross!

Surely he hath borne our infirmities and carried our sorrows. [45]

Arriving in Golgotha, it is still not enough for Him! He lays himself down and is nailed to the cross, to show His Bride that in every need, in every pain He is always there for her! It is actually not His cross but hers to which He is nailed! What can we say about the three-hour-agony, about the terrible abandonment!

My God, my God, why hast thou abandoned me? [46]

A woman had a dream one night that she had been abandoned by God. That was such coldness, loneliness and darkness that she woke up with a scream in her bed. After that she did not want to go back to sleep for days because she was afraid to have this same dream again!

Greater love than this no one has, that one lay down his life for his friends. [47]

Even His death was not enough for Him to show His love! It was still His will to let the soldier pierce His side and open His heart! That was also the moment where the Church was

---

[45] Is 53,4
[46] Mt 27,46
[47] Jn 15,13

born from His side, just as Eve was created from the side of the first Adam in the history of creation. His "hour" was the birth of the Church!

In the Passion of Christ a wonderful love occurs in time! This love is poured into the hearts of husbands in the sacrament of matrimony *because the charity of God is poured in our hearts by the Holy Ghost who has been given to us.*[48] **Husbands have a share in the love of Christ for His Church in this sacrament. Even if the husband can never be the savior of his wife, for this honor is only attributed to Jesus Christ alone, he can at least show the love of Christ to his wife. Remember that the spouses from Cana continued their wedding feast with the wine Jesus had given them.**

Love of Christ for His Bride in His Resurrection, Ascension and the descent of the Holy Ghost

Even His Resurrection was for our sake!

Who was delivered up for our sins, and rose again for our justification. [49]

But was not at least the Ascension just for Him?

In my Father's house there are many mansions. Were it not so, I should have told you, because I go to prepare a place for you.[50]

Even this triumph of the Ascension is connected to the welfare of his Church.

But does He at least have His peace and quiet in heaven? Yes and no!

Therefore He is able at all times to save those who come to God through Him, since He lives always to make intercession for them. [51]

---

[48] Rom 5,5
[49] Rom 4,25
[50] Jn 14,2
[51] Heb 7,25

In His life with the Father, resplendent with glory and honor, He never forgets the cares and worries of His Bride. He is always there for her to intercede before the Father.

On Pentecost, He has filled His Church with His spirit and His life. With that, He has sent the personal love of God, the Holy Ghost. St. Bernard takes the verse of the Canticle of Canticles *Let him kiss me with the kiss of his mouth!*[52] as fulfilled in the feast of Pentecost and the descent of the Holy Ghost. God, the Holy Ghost binds the Father and the Son in an unimaginable and magnificent love. This love found in the innermost being of the heart of God, is like a kiss. On Pentecost, this love comes like a *mighty storm*[53] and forms tongues of fire in descending down onto the Church. How invigorating is this love for the Church! Before that, the apostles, full of terror, had sat long hours hiding inside the cenacle. Barely did the "mighty storm" of the Holy Ghost descend upon them, they bravely went out on the street and proclaimed the crucified Jesus Christ! A husband, who is irritated with the boring and empty facial expression of his wife, could ask himself if he bestows the love that she needs and that he has promised her.

Love of Christ for His Bride in His Ministry

However, Jesus Christ has shown His love to His Bride not only in His earthly life, His prayers, His sacrifices and sufferings, but also by sharing His life's achievement with her. He has not simply lived and suffered for her, but He also entrusted so much to her.

First of all, his preaching:

Go, therefore, and make disciples of all nations![54] *He, who hears you, hears me!*[55] The Church teaches with the authority of Jesus Christ, not just with her own authority. She proclaims the Word of God in His place.

---

[52] Cant 1,2
[53] Acts 2,2
[54] Mt 28,19
[55] Lk 10,16

He has entrusted to her the children of God. *Feed my lambs, feed my sheep!*[56] They are so precious and valuable in His eyes and He is so much attached to them that He has readily given His life for them.

Greater love than this no one has, that one lay down his life for his friends![57]

Those children of God, he has entrusted them to his Church.

In this love, the husband also entrusts his children to his wife. A certain young man once said thoughtfully: "I ask myself if she could ever be the mother of my children."

Jesus has laid His offices in the hands of the Church: His power to teach and sanctify and govern. These offices are given deliberately to the Church as a sign of love. She participates in His life's work through these ministries. How much does He let her decide, let her do the structuring! The way to teach, the order of liturgy, the decisions over the path their children are to take, the building of the houses of God, the life of the religious, the missions, the catechism, the prayers and many more things. Here one can see that authority and to be the head does not mean to decide things alone. It is much nicer to delegate the duties because therein lies a unique kind of love, sympathy and participation.

> **That is also a guide for a Christian family: To be a father does not mean he must be like a commanding general. The mother and wife is involved in making decisions and he entrusts or delegates many things to her. If she is better in organizing the finances or in planning the vacation, why should she not do it? But she is doing it for him just as the Church is doing it for Christ.**

We especially wish to mention Confession here. Jesus has come to the world in order to save us from our sins.[58] On

---

[56] Jn 21,15
[57] Jn 15,13
[58] Mt 1,21

Good Friday, He gave up His life to repair for and forgive our sins.

> *But he was wounded for our iniquities, he was bruised for our sins. The chastisement of our peace was upon him, and by his bruises we are healed.*[59]

The work of the forgiveness of sins was in a way completed through His Resurrection on Easter morning, for He is risen *for our justification.*[60] Soon after Easter He gives this tremendous power of remitting sins which has cost Him so much, in the hands of His beloved Bride:

> *Receive the Holy Ghost; whose sins you shall forgive, they are forgiven them; and whose sins you shall retain, they are retained* [61]

Since then it is the great joy of the Church to grant the forgiveness of God together with Jesus in the sacrament of Penance. Here we can see that the Church participates in the central life work of Jesus: To give forgiveness and divine life. That means a supreme honor for the Church: The Savior of the world, the Redeemer of all ages wants his beloved Church by His side, when He practices His main office.

> *All glorious is the king's daughter as she enters; her raiment is threaded with spun of gold. In embroidered apparel, she is borne in to the king; behind her the virgins of her train are brought to you. They are borne in with gladness and joy; they enter the palace of the king.* [62]

So, Jesus wants His bride, the Church, to be by His side. Likewise, the husband should let his wife have a share in all important things possible. We do not live in a religion where the wife has to always walk one meter behind the husband. This common life of Christ and the Church, this participation of the Church in the life of Jesus Christ, finds its zenith in the Holy Mass, which we will talk about later. However, we should first see

---

[59] Is 53,5
[60] Rom 4,25
[61] Jn 20,22
[62] Ps 45,14ff

what is the reply of the Bride, the Church, on the love of her Groom.

The Catholic Church, the Bride of Jesus Christ

Standing in front of the sea or in front of a lake on a summer day, one is fascinated again and again how the sunlight is mirrored in thousands of little reflections from the waves. That is a portrait of the love of the Church with which she answers to the love of the Divine Heart of Jesus. The love of all Christians and all the saints is an answer to the burning love of Jesus Christ. The unfailing and unfathomable love of Christ is reflected and shines a thousand times, a million times back to heaven. Some people wonder why the Church especially celebrates the feast of St. Stephen. It may seem to be a stray feast day of a saint that was set on December 26 by accident. Yet it was intentionally placed there by the Church: The Son of God has come with an undying love at Christmas. The Church gives to her Groom the first Christian who gave his life for the newborn Savior as an answer to His love. St. Stephen was the first martyr and the Church offers him like a rose to the Child Jesus in the manger.

The next day, December 27, the Church celebrates the feast of St. John, who has understood the love of the Redeemer like no other men. He has named himself only *the disciple whom Jesus loved* and he is the one who rested at the breast of the Lord in the last supper. The Church expresses her love for Jesus Christ also in this feast. What else is Christ looking for other than recognition and response of His love?

I have come to cast fire upon the earth, and what will I but that it be kindled?[63]

Such is the love of a wife: a response to the love of her husband. In him, she always sees Christ, the Groom of the Church and His undying love to His Bride. In the

---

[63] Lk 12,49

> sacrament of matrimony, she indeed participates in the role of the Church as a bride of Jesus Christ and thereby, taking part in her vision of Christ. *The love of God is poured in our hearts!* These words of St. Paul also apply to the wife who loves her husband in Christ and through him, Our Lord Jesus Christ. She also drinks the wine of Cana and through that renews and refreshes her love. Whatever good she does to her husband, she does to Jesus.

The Church greets Jesus immediately with the gift of her love at Christmas. How could we describe all the love that the Church has given to Christ all these years! Those people who have given up their lives for Jesus Christ, who have wholly lived in His service, who have searched Him in silence and solitude, who have gone to answer His calling and have served Him in humility, chastity, poverty, simplicity, loyalty, obedience and perfect charity: they are the tips of the waves in which the ray of Divine Love is reflected!

For this purpose the Church has served Jesus Christ and His life work. She lives totally for Him, fulfills His orders, celebrates the sacrifice of the cross, extends His kingdom, advocates for His honor, defends his rights, and carries with him the cross. Already in the first three centuries the Church was flooded with waves of persecution, which brought death and martyrdom. It was only in the time of emperor Constantine that peace prevailed to some extent. Until then she had to show Jesus her loyalty and love by risking her life. She knows no other than Him.

> *For I am determined not to know anything among you, except Jesus Christ and him crucified.*[64]
>
> *Nay more, I count everything loss because of the excelling knowledge of Jesus Christ, my Lord. For his sake I have suffered the loss of all things, and I count them as dung that I may gain Christ.*[65]

---

[64] 1 Cor 2,2
[65] Phil 3,8

She has no independent career of her own, no projects, and no ambitions except for Him. If some of her servants act in a manner that is egotistic and selfish or greedy of power, it is clearly against the disposition and intention of the Church. It is not in her attitude and mission and therefore she is not responsible for the misdemeanor of her servants.

Therefore, the wife lives totally for her husband and not just beside him! She does not have her own career that makes her independent of him, because he too, lives totally for her and puts her in first place. His job only takes second place! Christ is the Head in favor of the Church and that gives her the strength to live totally for Him.

The Church gives to Jesus all her faithful, that is, her children. The Church has no intention to have her children only for herself; they belong more to Him than to her. By taking care of the faithful, she wants to lead children of God to Jesus. If she goes after the sinners and does not rest until they reach their eternal home, it is because they are the children of grace and belong to Jesus Christ.

Therefore, the mother does not keep her children for herself but for her husband. "I have given my husband up to concentrate totally on my children. That's enough for me!" These words of a family mother mean a declaration of bankruptcy in view of the original idea of a marriage. By that, she has given up the stand of the Church, to give Christ her faithful. In another chapter, we will talk about how can one deal with the limits, imperfections and failings of a spouse in marriage.

For an impression of how the Church lives wholly for Christ, simply look at the atmosphere and the spirit in a church.

When we enter, we observe calm and silence. Nothing should distract from the presence of Jesus. The whole structure of the church is focused on the altar and the tabernacle. Hence, our attention is again on Jesus Christ. The decorations of the church are there for him and to move the members of the Church to prayer and reverence, faith and devotion. The liturgy that is to be celebrated shows thousands of signs of adoration, respect, and love: Prayer, genuflection, bowing, incense, hymns, posture. Everything breathes a spirit of attentiveness, recollection and devotion.

These are exactly an expression of the Church's attitude towards her Groom. She lives wholly for Jesus, always in line with Him.

> **Following this example, the wife imitates the convictions and the principles of the Church. She tries her best to be always there for her husband, as he does also for her, in the imitation of Christ. Finally, the spouses are a symbol of Christ and the Church in the sacrament of Matrimony. This symbol should remind us of the Divine Spouses by living spiritually the life of this Couple.**

This bearing of the Church is seen even more clearly in Mary. Her way of living is exactly in conformity to the convictions and principles of the Church. She plays a central role in the Church and cannot be separated from her. Her faith (i.e. her thinking in mind and spirit with Christ), her humility and charity are an epitome of a bridal devotion to Christ.

Everything that the faith and Marian devotions are trying to say about the Blessed Virgin Mary finds its echo accordingly in the Church. The *great sign,* in which the Church is dressed with the sun in the 12th chapter of the Apocalypse[66], is interpreted as both the Church and the Blessed Virgin Mary.

---

[66] Apoc. 12,1f

> For a wife, a deep devotion to Mary is an easy and simple way to find the right convictions and attitudes in marriage.

The Head and the Body

He is the head of his body, the Church.[67]

Christ and the Church stand side-by-side and live together as the Head and the Body. There are different kinds of authority: the teacher over his students, the general over the soldiers, the government over the people, and the parents toward their children. A special kind of authority is found between the Head and the Body; this is very different from the examples mentioned above. Eve was formed from Adam's body, taken from his side and put by his side as an extension of his life, so to speak. This origin has stamped the relation between a man and a woman.

For man was not created for woman, but woman for man.[68]

Similarly, the Church is created for the sake of Our Lord Jesus Christ. These basic principles dictate the mutual relationship between Christ and the Church, and between husband and wife. Christ and the Church live with each other and for each other.

Our Lord Jesus Christ is the Head of the Church, in favor of the Church, who in turn lives for Him.

For the Son of Man also has not come to be served but to serve, and to give his life as a ransom for many.[69]

Jesus is the King of kings, everything is created for Him, and He is the Alpha and Omega, the Son of God, sharing the same nature with His Father, Redeemer of the world.

---

[67] Col. 1,18
[68] 1 Cor 11,9
[69] Mk 10,45

Knowing this, we must be amazed at the manner in which He has chosen to be the Head of the Church.

The Roman Catechism adds to that:

For the apostle instructs this rule saying: 'Husbands love your wives, as Christ has loved the Church,' which comprises an immeasurable love, not for his own gain, but keeping always in his mind only to the advantage of his Bride.[70]

At the Last Supper, He left His apostles His Testament and showed them again how ready He is to serve them. In full awareness of His dignity and magnitude *(Jesus, knowing that the Father had given all things in his hands, and that he had come forth from God and was going to God*[71]*)*, rose from the supper and bent His knees to wash the feet of the apostles. Afterwards, He said to them:

You call me Master and Lord, and you say well, for so I am. If therefore, I the Lord and Master have washed your feet, you also ought to wash the feet of one another. For I have given you an example, that as I have done to you, so you should also do.

That shows us how and in what manner Jesus is the Head of his Church. He is the Head in favor of her. He is the Head not for his own sake, but for the sake of his Body. It should then be emphasized, that being the Head is a gift to his Church, for he practices it only to her advantage. Far from letting her serve him, he made himself the servant of his Church.

If the husband is the head of his wife, he should fulfill his duties in that same manner: for her benefit. It is necessary to emphasize this because there are so many clichés that darken the understanding of Christian marriage. There are these words of Scripture that always seem to be emphasized by many: *Let women be subject to their husbands.* **That is correct, these words are from St. Paul, yet that is not all! Another word is left unconsidered:** *Husbands, love your wives as Christ loves the*

---

[70] Catechism of the Council of Trent, II, ch. 8, q.22
[71] Jn 13,3ff

Church and has given up Himself for her, that is, serving her with dedication and devotion until the end of his life. Was this not an occasion for today's emancipatory movement to exaggerate and distort the notions of paternal authority in marriage and family!

Although the husband is the head of the wife, he is not the head in order to be served. On the contrary, he is there to lead and to give her his love. As soon as this is correctly observed, the artificial argument, "Who will be the master over whom?" is solved. For which wife would not be willing to submit to a husband who loves her and whose love she knows?

This submission of the wife to her husband applies to the common family life, but not to the matter of their mutual love and relationship. Here, both stand on the same level.

Can we imagine the Church constantly working against the intentions of Christ? Or putting herself above his level, and commanding him? Or acting independently of Christ? This impression is made by a wife, who in fact takes the role of the Church, but acts constantly against her husband's will or tries to take over her husband's role to rule and lead the family. How much disturbance is there in some families because this natural order of life is not observed! There is no sense in pointing out whose fault it is, rather both should try to make a new start by following the right order of things.

On the other hand, can we imagine Our Lord Jesus Christ pausing in carrying out His responsibilities for His Church and giving up His duty as the Head of the Church? Many husbands abandon their office and "take a break" or resign. The outcome is quickly noticeable. Love grows cold and the family becomes "headless;" disorder and chaos in the long run are inevitable. Experience shows the roots of many serious family problems lie here.

In the Gospel, the servant was severely punished who did not do something with the talent his master had entrusted him. In the end he wanted to give it back without any fruits.

Wicked and slothful servant!... But from the unprofitable servant, cast him forth into the darkness outside, where there will be the weeping, and the gnashing of teeth.[72]

The Common Life of Christ and the Church

Above all, Head and Body have a common life and each takes part in the other. With great love, Christ has a share in the life of the Church, in her joys, in her sufferings, in her persecutions, in her concerns and petitions. He has even promised to fulfill all her wishes:

And whatever you ask in my name, that I will do...[73]

A thought-provoking impulse for husbands! When she is persecuted, it is a persecution of His own Person:

Saul, Saul why are you persecuting me?[74]

When she is happy, He is also happy with her:

Rejoice with those who rejoice, and weep with those who weep.[75]

He sees every tear from her eyes: *and God will wipe away every tear from their eyes.*[76]

Most of all, He takes part in her pains and carries her cross:

Surely he has borne our infirmities and carried our sorrows.[77]

---

[72] Mt 25,26f
[73] Jn 14,13
[74] Acts 22,7
[75] Rom 12,15
[76] Apoc. 7,17
[77] Is 53,4

He not only participates in the life of His Church, but He also gives the Church a share in His life: In the state of grace, she takes part in His Divine Nature. In the Holy Ghost who is her soul, she is sharing the life of the Son of God. In the faith, she is of one thought with her Groom, Jesus Christ; in the Gifts of the Holy Ghost, she is introduced deep into His thoughts and affections; in hope, she already participates in His eternal and immeasurable bounty; in charity, she is with Him in God and God in her. Is it not amazing how Christ lets His bride participate in His Divine life? He has placed her as the queen by His side! What kind of love is this!

Together with Him, the Church lives for the glorification of the Father. It is His everything to glorify the Father. This is also the greatest and deepest concern of the Church. That is why she builds monasteries and Churches, goes into missions, builds schools and seminaries, supports the families and does so many things in an abundant field of work!

He makes her share the deepest mysteries of His Sacred Heart.

But I have called you friends, because all things that I have heard from my Father I have made known to you.[78]

To you it is given to know the mysteries of the kingdom of heaven.[79]

Together with Him, she sanctifies the children of God in the sacraments, especially in Confession. Jesus would not forgive sins that are not forgiven by the Church. That is why the giving of His absolution depends on her:

Receive the Holy Spirit; whose sins you shall forgive, they are forgiven them; and whose sins you shall retain, they are retained.[80]

The climax of this mutual participation is reached in the celebration of Holy Mass: Every Holy Mass is indeed a work of

---

[78] Jn 15,15
[79] Mt 13,11
[80] Jn 20,22f

the Church, not only of the persons present. That means a true presence of the bride of Christ, who is united to the Groom, Jesus Christ. Our Lord lays down His entire life's work in the hands of the Church! On the other hand, she unites her whole life, her total existence, her crosses, joys, worries, petitions, and thoughts with those of her Groom. They stand together before the Father and He blesses them in infinite bounty. Here she listens to His word and He listens to her prayers. Here he thinks of her and she of him. Here they share an inexhaustible deepness of common life! Here he shows his love through the everlasting renewal of his Passion on the Cross, his devotion for her! Here she brings all her love and joins in the flames of Divine Love.

But he who is joined to the Lord, is one spirit.[81]

It is an enormous honor for the Church when at the end of the Canon in the Mass, she may offer the endless adoration of Christ together with Our Lord Jesus Christ Himself!

Per ipsum et cum ipso at in ipso est tibi Deo omnipotenti in unitate Spiritus Sancti omnis honor et gloria. – Through Him, in Him, with Him there is rendered to Thee, God the Father Almighty, in the unity of the Holy Ghost all honor and glory.

We find here the Church and Our Lord Jesus Christ inseparably united. It is unimaginable for them to not stay together forever. Likewise, a divorce for Christian spouses is unimaginable.

If we think about it, Christ and the Church renew their bond in the celebration of the Holy Mass. For the first Adam was in a deep sleep when God created Eve from his side to be his wife. When Christ's side was opened and water and blood poured out, His Bride, the Church, was born. That moment was the birth of the Church. If the Holy Mass is the renewal of the Passion on the Cross, then it is also the realization of the birth of the Church from the pierced side of Christ. Therefore,

---

[81] 1 Cor 6,17

it follows that Christ and His Church strengthen and renew their eternal union in the Holy Mass.

This is so encouraging for the married spouses! If they attend the Holy Mass, they come back to the origin of their marriage. The branch meets the trunk! Just as the trunk strengthens its life in the Mass, so is also the Christian marriage renewed and revived in the Mass. Here, at the altar, Christ gives the better wine of Cana, in which the spouses can continue their marriage in holy joy and deep security.

I am the vine, you are the branches. He who abides in me, and I in him, he bears much fruit: for without me you can do nothing.[82]

For the charity of Christ presses us.[83]

It impels the married couples to live after what can be found in Christ and the Church. They must live after this love, this sympathy, this living for each other. The same love, the same reciprocity and the same order of things should be found in them!

In the Holy Mass, Christ and the Church carry the cross together throughout time. The spouses also take part in it.

Archbishop Lefebvre has said, *What accounts for the power of Catholic marriages is that both can direct their glance on the Holy Sacrifice of the Mass and know that marriage is also a cross. Marriage must be founded on the Sacrifice of the Holy Mass, which is the renewal of Our Lord's Passion on the Cross. Hence, they will carry the difficulties of marriage together... The moment we set aside the sacrifice and the cross, we will inevitably fall into sin.*[84]

---

[82] Jn 15, 5
[83] 2 Cor 5,14
[84] Sermon to future deacons, June 1, 1990.

In the Holy Mass, we can see clearly once again, how Christ and the Church stand before each other. If we ask in the liturgy, "Who is leading whom?" it is then obvious that it is Our Lord Jesus Christ who leads the Church and that the Church submits to Him. He loves her, He has given His life for her, but He is indeed the Head.

Thus, attending Mass is an opportunity for a married couple to renew this spirit of order in marriage that God has willed for them.

Life for their Children

Jesus Christ and His Bride have one goal: The glorification of God and the salvation and sanctification of souls. Everything we have discussed about the common works of both, is directed to this double goal.

> *I came that they may have life, and have it more abundantly. I am the good shepherd. The good shepherd lays down his life for his sheep.* [85]

It is His will to give His life to the children of God, His brothers and sisters in the Holy Catholic Church. He wants this divine life to develop, grow, and finally bring everyone to the House of the Father, from which it is stated:

> *Eye has not seen or ear heard, nor it has entered into the heart of man, what things God has prepared for those who love him.* [86]

As we have seen, the Church stands side-by-side with the Redeemer of the world as a loyal companion in this work.

The children of God shall live in this glorious eternal city one day, which is the Church herself:

> *And there came one of the seven angels who had the bowls full of the seven last plagues; and he spoke with me, saying, 'Come, I will show thee the bride, the spouse of the Lamb.' And he took me up in spirit to a mountain, great and high, and showed me*

---

[85] Jn 10,10f
[86] 1 Cor 2,9

the holy city Jerusalem, coming down out of heaven from God, having the glory of God. Its light was like to a precious stone, as it were a jasper stone, clear as a crystal. And it had a wall great and high with twelve gates, and at the gates twelve angels, and names written on them, which are the names of the twelve tribes of the children of Israel. On the east are three gates, and on the north three gates, and on the south three gates, and on the west three gates. And the wall of the city has twelve foundation stones, and on them twelve names of the twelve apostles of the Lamb. And he who spoke with me had a measure, a golden reed, to measure the city and the gates thereof and the wall. And the city stands foursquare, and its length is as great as its breadth; and he measured the city with the reed, to twelve thousand stadia: the length and the height of it are equal. And he measured its wall, of a hundred and forty-four cubits, man's measure, that is, angel's measure. And the material of its wall was jasper; but the city itself was pure gold, like pure glass. And the foundations of the wall of the city were adorned with every precious stone. The first foundation, jasper; the second, sapphire; the third, agate; the fourth, emerald; the fifth, sardonyx; the sixth, sardius; the seventh, chrysolite; the eighth, beryl; the ninth, topaz; the tenth, chrysoprase; the eleventh, jacinth; the twelfth, amethyst. And the twelve gates were twelve pearls; that is, each gate was of a single pearl. And the street of the city was pure gold, as it were transparent glass. And I saw no temple therein, For the Lord God Almighty and the Lamb are the temple thereof. And the city has no need for the sun or the moon to shine upon it. For the glory of God lights it up, and the Lamb is the lamp thereof. And the nations shall walk by the light thereof; and the kings of the earth shall bring their glory and honor into it. And its gates shall not be shut by day; for there shall be no night there. And they shall bring the glory and the honor of nations into it.[87]

In a Christian family, father and mother pray and work for this great and overwhelming goal, if they are there for the children day and night. Sometimes it is unutterably hard to be a parent. That is exactly when they need

---

[87] Rev 21,9ff

this perspective on the eternal goal, to which they are to bring up the beloved children, whom God entrusted them. The thought of the immortal souls and the eternal destiny of their own children is an enormous source of strength for the parents!

Christ and the Church cooperate together especially in the sanctification of the priests. This for several reasons.

The well-being of the faithful depends on the sanctity of the priest. There is the principle: "Like the shepherd, so the flock." A bad priest can be cause of great harm and can lead many souls to hell. On the other hand, a good priest can lead many, many children of God, children of Christ and the Church, to heaven. Saint John Baptist Vianney, the Curé of Ars, heard over 100,000 confessions in his lifetime and was very effective. For many, the encounter with this simple priest was a turning point in their life that brought them infinite, unutterable happiness in heaven.

Therefore, when Christ and the Church give special care to the priests, this has a deep meaning for the children of God.

A further reason is found in the nature of the priesthood. Through his consecration and his priestly character, the priest is an agent of the Church and an agent of Christ. It is sometimes so fascinating to see in a children's face both parents, father's and also mother's face. In the priest, you can also see the visage of Christ and the Church who want to work through him. As the child in a marriage is a pledge of mutual love, the divine couple finds the bond of mutual love in the priest. In him both are acting together, in him they are giving each other their mutual love; just think of his special role at Mass.

However, the priest is not just the expression of the mutual love of both; he also acts in their name. What else should he do but to be completely absorbed in the prayer and action of Christ and the Church? This too is why they have such joy in priesthood.

In this sense, the Christian family should show a great love for the priesthood, because between them there is a deep connection. How beautiful it is, when during family prayer, we think about the priests! Maybe this point should play a much greater part in a family's prayer life.

Living out the Sacrament of Matrimony

After we have meditated on the master copy of matrimony, we will now consider how the living of the sacrament is accomplished. It is stated in the introduction to the wedding of Cana that, *Three days later there was a wedding feast at Cana, in Galilee; and Jesus' mother was there. Jesus himself and His disciples had also been invited.* Jesus, Mary and the apostles were present at the wedding. Likewise, Our Lord Jesus Christ is also present in a Christian marriage according to his words:

For there where two or three gather together for my sake, there am I in the midst of them.[88]

What determines the marriage life in the sacrament? It is the fact that Catholic marriage is a sign for Christ and the Church, and a living symbol with intimate, supernatural and real affiliation to the original.

Hence, a Catholic married couple lives as a symbol. A symbol must be clear and distinct. If we see flashing lights on the road, it is immediately clear that an emergency vehicle is coming. If we see a signpost, we know that what is written on it will give clear directions. Even St. Paul points out the need for a symbol to be clear:

Even lifeless instruments, like the flute or the harp, may produce sound, but if there is no difference in the notes, how shall it be known what is piped or harped? And if the trumpet gives forth an uncertain sound, who will prepare for battle?[89]

---

[88] Mt 18,20
[89] 1 Cor 14,7f

Married couples who are living together only as colleagues, or are merely united out of pure natural ties, or who have given up mutual love, give such an unclear message. It is also a blurry message when the husband lets his responsibility for his wife and family slip, because he has given the lead of the family into the hands of his wife. It is also a conflicting signal when the spouses are constantly arguing, perhaps even in front of the children. We could even go on to make a long list of examples but that is not necessary. It simply depends on the question: Are we striving each day to live like the Eternal Bride and Groom and in that way imitate them, or have we given up this fight for the growth of our love?

It is indeed important to be reminded of Christ and the Church by the Christian married couple. This happens through their similarity of love, of mutual respect, of the sympathy they have for each other, and of the common goal. Just as the origin of the wine of Cana is not from this world (the chief steward could not determine its origin), so it should also be with the love that is to be found among married couples. It is supposed to be exactly the same love that lives between Christ and the Church. That is far more than just natural sympathy and attachment.

To be clear, this means that the husband should often meditate on how diverse and rich the love is that Christ has for His Church. He must be familiar with it and try to mold his life according to that fashion. In prayer and in the sacraments he will find the strength to do it, especially in the sacrament of matrimony itself, where the wine of Cana is constantly poured anew into the heart.

The wife fulfills her duty as the representative of the Church, as she is the living pillar of devotion in the marriage as that which the Church shows Christ. What good she does to her husband, she does to Christ. For her too this applies: she must be familiar with the example of the Church. We cannot imitate what we do not know. Her source of strength is the same as that of her husband, the sacrament of matrimony itself and a good prayer life, especially a deep devotion to the Blessed Virgin Mary.

On the other hand, there are also some distinct differences from the eternal Bride and Groom; above all, the husband and father is not the savior of his wife and children. The father is not a priest. That is why the matter of redemption is reserved to Our Lord Jesus Christ alone. However, there is no doubt that the father should pray for his wife and children and that he should carry the cross for them and with them.

The living out of the sacrament of matrimony is the living of a supernatural life. That is why it needs a special source of strength and special attention. Without the regular habit of praying together, regular confession and communion, it is not possible to bear good fruits. Attending Mass, especially, preferably together, is an indispensable requirement for the sacramental life to survive.[90]

Much is already said in the above paragraph. Nevertheless, some points have still to be mentioned specifically. The reader should keep in mind the warning that we have spoken about in the foreword: They must live a life corresponding to reality, as opposed to roles like in a play.

Signs of Love

It is oftentimes overlooked that the imitation of love of Christ requires signs of love. Here is a little example of a story that at first glance looks a bit strange but actually often corresponds to real life:

There lived two friends with their families in a village as neighbors. Everybody knew that Steve and Robert had been best friends for years. They went to kindergarten and school together. When Robert, coming out of his house, saw Steve

---

[90] "You can say in all truth: The spouses who frequently assist at the renewal of the sacrifice of the Cross, that is at the renewal of the wedding of Our Lord and his Church, revive the grace of their marriage and increase that special grace they need to fulfill as true Christians what is demanded of them in marriage. They have to assist at Holy Mass. Holy Mass is really the foundation of a Christian family. The Church wants it this way." Archb. M. Lefebvre, Easter retreat, 1980.

working in his garden, he would not greet him; after all, it was clear that they were good friends. Steve was busy working in his garden, in which, by the way, fewer and fewer flowers grew.

One day an ambulance stood in front of Robert's house, but Steve did not ask what had happened to his friend; after all, it was indeed clear that he stood always by his side. A few days later, they met on the street and did not talk about the ambulance, but rather talked about the weather, for both agreed that it was not worthwhile to talk about that incident. When the son of Steve graduated at last from his apprenticeship and the family hosted a barbecue party in the garden, no one from Robert's family went; after all, it was clear that everybody was happy about it. Thus, the years passed by and they lived side by side, the best of friends. One thing was noticeable; their gardens grew more barren.

At the end, Steve's garden had been tilled under and lawn grass planted everywhere, because that easier. Finally Robert went into retirement and invited some people to celebrate with him. It was not necessary to invite Steve; after all, he was happy anyways for his friend's well-earned retirement. In the meantime, both were over 70 and were already too old to change anything! What could have been changed? And so Steve died (Robert had no interest in attending the burial; he prayed for Steve at home) and in time Robert died. But they had been a whole lifelong the best of friends!

We apologize, dear reader, for presenting such a weird story! However, many marriages present such a strange picture. There is only one distinct element in the whole story that makes everything odd: The absence of signs of friendship! Friendship was here but the signs of friendship were missing! And that alone makes things unrealistic.

Fr. Dantec had met hundreds of married couples in France and served as spiritual director to these families for more than 15 years. He wrote in his book *Voyez comme ils s'aiment* about the signs of love in marriage: *It is always a damage of a greatest kind when the signs of love are missing in marriage.* He calls it a "very great damage" indeed!

What does he mean by the gestures of love? *Loving glances, tender words, caresses, a shoulder to lean on, holding the spouse's hand, putting the arms around the shoulders, confidential words.* Hence, these are gestures, which from nature itself are not sensual. They do not belong to the realms of sexuality but serve as expressions of mutual love. In how many marriages are these signs of love missing? And it seems that exactly in these marriages the relationship between spouses is as it were depressed and paralyzed. No wonder it is as a matter of fact a "very great damage" for the marriage, when one thinks love can survive without these gestures. The marital relationship will surely be like the story of Steve and Robert.

As time goes by, it happens so easily that these gestures are omitted. In the beginning, one thinks that everything is clear and obvious. Or a small argument occurs and we use coldness as a weapon. Or one thinks he or she should be "realistic" (realistic in the way of a worldly two-stage-marriage). In any case, these signs and gestures gradually subside and it does not matter for a while. However, the love affair will soon be but a strange affair!

If he or she now considers which of them should make the first move to start again with these signs of love, then that is like someone who is choking, but speculating if he should first breathe in or breathe out...!

Thus, the love among people lives in these signs and gestures. In marriage the same love, the same reciprocity, and the same order of things should be expressed as between Christ and the Church! Both have given each other thousand gestures and signs of love:

Think about the wounds of Jesus, His consolations, His answers to prayers, everything we have said above. Is not the decoration of a Church, the reverences and the prayers in the liturgy, the acts of charity, the silence in the Church, the life of the religious a sign of love to Our Lord Jesus Christ? With what respect, with what esteem and attachment do Christ and the Church approach each other! This respect, this acknowledgment and unity should also be found among Catholic married couples. If we see them, it should remind us of Christ and the Church just as the grapes speak of the vine!

Imagine for a moment, if the Church did not celebrate the Holy Mass anymore, the tabernacle was put aside, the churches were neglected and the feast days omitted; if the priests only lived for money and pleasures, the faithful did not pray or make sacrifices anymore, etc. It would be the worst crisis of the Church and it would have come so from the missing signs of love!

So married couples have to decide whether they go on omitting the signs and gestures of love and decide not to belong to the Vine, Christ and the Church, and be like "spiritual bananas" … or more seriously put, rather be like the fruitless and dried up branch. They must be reminded of the spiritual reality and start again, give each other the better wine of Cana which is to be found in great abundance in the sacrament of matrimony. Yet they have to remember what kind of love they express in their gestures: That is the love of Christ and the Church! And so they have to be a musician of the heart! Then what a symphony is played in marriage, a song of the eternal Bride and Groom!

Forgiving is Living

To be a musician of the heart means also to go deal with the weakness, imperfections and limitations. How do we see it on the part of Jesus Christ? His bride is pure and holy but her members are not always! How do we see it on the part of the Church? Jesus Christ is the Son of God but he also appears to her in a very human form! The vine itself is very healthy but the branches are oftentimes so terribly trimmed, are sometimes dried out and bear strange fruits!

Now, from both we can take an example in difficult situations. All families are different and we cannot compare one marriage to another; however, the basic rules of Jesus Christ apply here:

Let him who is without sin among you be the first to cast a stone![91]

---

[91] Jn 8,7ff

> *Now the Scribes and Pharisees brought a woman caught in adultery, and setting her in the midst, said to him, "Master, this woman was even now taken in adultery. Now Moses in the law commanded us to stone such a one. But what sayest thou?" Now they were saying this to test him, in order that they might be able to accuse him. But Jesus, stooping down, began to write with his finger on the ground. But when they continued asking him, he raised himself and said to them, "Let him who is without sin among you be the first to cast a stone at her." And again stooping down, he began to write on the ground. But hearing this, they went away, one by one, beginning with the eldest. And Jesus remained alone, with the woman standing in the midst. And Jesus, raising himself, said to her, "Woman, where are they? Has no one condemned thee?" She said, "No one, Lord." Then Jesus said, "Neither will I condemn thee. Go thy way, and from now on sin no more!"*

Another very important basic principle of Our Lord Jesus Christ concerning human weakness:

> *Amen I say to you, as long as you did it for one of these, the least of my brethren, you did it for me.*[92]

This has a special meaning in a marriage because the link to Christ and the Church is special. What the spouses do to each other, they do to Christ and to the Church. In addition, Jesus has not said, "As long you did it for one of these, the holiest of my brethren, you did it for me," and neither "As long you did it for one of these, the most perfect of my brethren, you did it for me," but he said *the least of my brethren*.

The spouse stays always as a representative of Christ or of the Church, no matter what faults and weaknesses he or she has. We also know that from other usual "offices." We expect the children to be obedient and respectful towards their parents, even if the parents have faults and shortcomings. Or if a teacher drives too fast, he does not cease to be a teacher because of that. The sacrament of matrimony gives the spouses a kind of "sanctification" which they do not lose until death.

---

[92] Mt 25,40

Therefore, one must make a distinction: As a husband or as a wife he or she should always keep the love and respect, which Christ and the Church deserve. That is enormously great! As a human being with flaws, weaknesses and limitations, the other is always in the hands of God and in the heart of God. If there were a marriage crisis, which from time to time can happen, the situation would look much different if they would observe both these points!

Order and Structure

A married couple is a symbol of Christ and the Church through mutual love. However, not only through this love should they recall Christ and the Church but also through the manner in which they stand to each other. The Church stands at the side of Christ as his companion and puts herself under the Head. She acknowledges her subordination and she lets him lead her. He takes his responsibility for her and lovingly leads her. The question "who leads whom?" is totally clear and easy to answer. It would be madness for the Church if she made Christ obey her rules. This obedience is not like that of children to their parents but it corresponds exactly to her vocation as companion to Christ's side. At the same time, it should be emphasized that this subordination applies only to their common life and work. In matters of mutual love, there are no such things as subordination and dominance for they stand on the same level.

The nature of the trunk should also reflect in the branches of the supernatural vine. Because Catholic married couples are rooted in this trunk, and because they really live only from this trunk, the features of the Divine Bride and Groom must also be found in them. It is a permanent hindrance for the grace of the sacrament if a couple follows its "own model" in this point of order. Then they actually resist the life of Christ and the Church. One cannot expect the abundant fruits of grace to flow if this point is violated again and again. It should be made clear that the dominance of the wife over her husband gives the message that the Church rules over Christ and she is the one leading him...

How often do we find couples having this distorted order for years? Whenever the husband has not taken his responsibilities seriously and his position as head is "dormant," or perhaps the wife cannot bear that he did not fulfill her notions and expectations? In such a power struggle develops, instead of both taking again his or her rightful place. Consequently, they both live for themselves, beside the partner and not for each other. In many cases, it turns out to be a life against each other! That is a fast way to suffocate love!

It has severe consequences for the children, too. Apart from serious damage, it is a permanent bad example if children see their parents constantly arguing, a rebellious and manipulative mother or a negligent and irresponsible father. How will the children learn obedience if the mother is not able to submit herself to her husband? On the other hand, where will the loyalty of the children to obligation and responsibility stem from? The parents have constantly set different examples.

> *But whoever causes one of these little ones who believe in me to sin, it were better for him to have a great millstone hung around his neck, and to be drowned in the depths of the sea.*[93]

There is a famous definition of peace: *Peace is the tranquility of order*[94] There would be true peace in a marriage and family if the order of God is maintained. If man tries to replace the laws of God, chaos and disputes can only be the outcome.

There is only one case in which the wife has to take over the guidance of the family. Pope Pius XI said, *Degree and ways of submission of the wife under her husband can thereupon vary depending on the different personal, local and temporal conditions. If the husband will not perform his duties, it is even the responsibility of the wife to take his position in the managing of the family. But it's never and nowhere allowed to simply invert or to infringe the structure of the family and its confirmed basic laws attached to it that have been enacted by God.*[95] This case assumes a severe and persistent violation of duty on the part of the father. In all other cases, it

---

[93] Mt 18,6
[94] St. Augustine, De Civitate Dei, ch. 19.
[95] Pope Pius XI, Casti Connubii.

applies that the structure of the family can *"never and nowhere"* be overturned.

But what if the wife is more clever, more intelligent, more experienced than her husband? Should she not at least take over the spiritual management of the family?

Who was more intimately united with God in the Holy Family in Nazareth? Joseph or Mary? The answer is clear, and yet Mary has submitted herself to Joseph. Note well, the Child Jesus was the holiest member of the Family of Nazareth. Nevertheless, it is said about Jesus: *and He was subject to them.*[96] If the mutual arrangement were in order, then it would bring great blessings in marriage and in the family. It is as if a curtain is pushed aside and the sun shines brightly in the family. Because then nothing hinders the grace of God to flow. And so they find *love, happiness, peace, patience, gentleness, benevolence, loyalty and fidelity, meekness, temperance.*[97]

Here it should be emphasized once again that this question "Who leads whom?" applies only to the common life and duties, most of all, the children; but it is not applicable to the personal love life between spouses, where both are equal to each other.

On the other hand, this structure does not exclude the division of tasks and duties. As Christ has allowed His Church to make so many decisions (form of the liturgy, structure of missions, sermon and catechism, spiritual guidance of the children of God), so the mother of the family undertakes many things in accordance with her own dexterity and capability. She does it to complement her husband, not against him or beside him, but for him.

The Children

Not all marriages are blessed with children. That is often a hard trial of which God alone knows the pain. And yet such

---

[96] Lk 2,51
[97] Gal 5,22

marriages are far from ending up empty-handed. They are a great gift for the Church if they express the love, esteem and respect which Christ and the Church give to each other in their marriage. It can be a great encouragement for others if their love glows, a love that the world doesn't know and till old age still try to be like the eternal Bride and Groom.

If the parents give life to their children, they do it within the parameters of the sacrament of matrimony. Without them, the history of the Church would soon be ended! They give the Church always new branches in which the coming generations are reached.

These marriage acts must be characterized with mutual love and respect, which springs from the sacrament of matrimony.

> ...that every one of you learn how to possess his own wife in holiness and honor, not in the passion of lust like the Gentiles who do not know God.[98]

The same spirit breathes a passage in the book of Tobias, where it is spoken of a couple after the wedding:

> Then Tobias exhorted the virgin, and said to her: "Sara, arise, and let us pray to God today, and tomorrow and when the third night is over, we will be in our own wedlock. For we are the children of saints, and we must not be joined together like heathens that know not God." So they both arose, and prayed earnestly both together that health might be given them. And Tobias said: "Lord God of our fathers, may the heavens and the earth, and the sea, and the fountains, and the rivers, and all thy creatures that are in them, bless thee. Thou madest Adam of the slime of the earth, and gavest him Eve for a helper. And now, Lord, thou knowest that not for fleshly lust do I take my sister to wife, but only for the love of posterity, in which thy name may be blessed forever and ever."[99]

St. Paul has recommended abstaining from marriage act only at times:

---

[98] 1 Thess 4,4
[99] Tob 8,4ff

Do not deprive each other, except perhaps by consent, for a time, that you may give yourselves to prayer; and return together again lest Satan tempt you because you lack self-control.[100]

The independent refusal of the marriage act can lead to the ruin of a marriage, indeed all the way to hell.

This marriage act is willed by Our Creator and has an important role in the marriage relationship. St. Cyril of Jerusalem has said, *Nothing unclean is in the nature of man, except he stains himself through adultery and fornication. He, who has made Adam, has also made Eve. Man and woman are made from God's hands. None of the members was initially unclean by his creation. May the heretics fall silent who condemn the body or the Creator respectively.*[101]

Indeed one can sometimes be reminded of the beginning of creation and the words from the Genesis: *The earth was waste and void; darkness covered the abyss.*[102] The abyss that is mentioned here is a symbol for the restless sea of chaos, from which God formed creation. But over this restless chaos the Spirit of the Creator was stirring and was leading it to something higher. *The Spirit of God was stirring above the waters.* Such is also the marriage act ennobled through three values that make up the goods of marriage. St. Augustine enumerates them: the good of bearing a child, the good of faithfulness and the good of the sacrament.[103] This union indeed serves these three goals and takes up from here a high status. Only without these goals would the coming together be *waste and void*.

When the child is born, upbringing begins. Remember the great influence parents have on their children. In every generation, the influence of the parents is again found like a tint or a basic mood. We, humans cannot always rethink every situation, cannot follow every conclusion back up to the roots. It is impossible to recapture all values in every situation, to immediately and properly classify every situation, to take a

---

[100] 1 Cor 7,5
[101] St. Cyril of Jerusalem, 12. catech., chap 26
[102] Gen 1,2
[103] De bono coniugali 24,32, in: PL 40, 394

new stand each time. We are built up on our history and our experiences. So many thoughts, feelings, convictions, words and deeds come from what we have become so far and from what we have experienced. And the experiences we have had with our parents play a big role. We often decide on things according to what is obvious and familiar to us. It always costs us efforts to take foreign and new measures or standards. It is almost comparable to a riverbed; the river finds it hard to flow into another direction, even harder to flow to a different area.

Of course, a man can pursue with the help of grace a different rule of life than what he is used to. That is always bound with a burdensome effort and needs sacrifice and prayer. One is often tempted to fall back to the old pattern. If necessary, God gives his powerful grace and help to everybody for any new direction in life. After all, he has made Paul out of Saul! However, the normal way is that the parents set an example to their child in which he is oriented. In this process, words count less than the example of the parents. The parents always leave a deep impression on the emotional level, not only on the intellectual level. With that, the parents mold their children in two ways:

- On the level of creation, they are for the children an image and likeness of God,
- On the level of redemption, they are for the children an image of Christ and the Church.

However, what does the gospel contain, what does the catechism contain, if not the message of God, Christ and the Church? The parents are a living example that leads to God without so many words. For an image is always here to lead it to its original.

Before we go to this twofold illustration of the character of parents, the example of Martin Luther should be presented. It shows how the influence of parents can be profoundly deep.

Martin Luther had an overly strict father. *For a small nut's sake I was beaten with rods until blood was flowing,* he wrote. After these beatings, the young Martin did not dare to be near his father for weeks. No wonder the father appeared to him indiscriminately strict and unpredictable at the same time. We want to compare that with his experience at his first Mass. On May 2, 1507, he celebrated his first Mass. As he was about to pray the words of the offertory: *Accept, O Holy Father, almighty and eternal God*, he was then overcome with such dread terror that he wished to leave the altar. A fellow priest had to convince him to stay and finish the Mass.

What binds both events is the father figure. Luther saw almighty God according to the image that he had of his father: here was an overly strict God Who was unpredictable and could instill fear. He said on this circumstance: *Who was I, that I might address such a terrible Majesty!* Because of this distorted view of God, he tried to attain that feeling of having pleased God through years of penance and sacrifice. Since he did not succeed, he fell later into despair, concluding that a man stays always a "soiled fellow" and God just constantly covers the existing sins.

In view of this context, one can ask oneself if the history of Europe would have been different if Martin Luther had had a more moderate father, who in his strictness also had kept the right sense of judgment... Do fathers nowadays know what comes from them for the coming generations...?

The Parents as the image and likeness of the Creator

We, human beings are created in the image and likeness of God. An image is there to present something (the master copy, perhaps a tree), to be viewed and to lead the viewer to the original. The parents are also created as an image and likeness of God. They are the first image of God for the children. From the kindness, honesty, love, patience and humility of the parents they learn the first notions of these attributes in God.

The experience of pastoral care offers hundreds of examples, what the existence or absence of these values in parents means to the next generation. A young child is quite set out to learn these things from his parents. If young Guido says, "My daddy can do everything!" he has not become thoroughly insane but he has simply seen the image of the Almighty in his father...

The Creator comes to meet us in different ways:
- He has created us out of nothing,
- He keeps us in existence,
- He helps us to bring our abilities into action, and
- He takes care of us through his Divine Providence.

God's creation from nothing has a parallel in respect that the parents give life to their child. Also in later years, it is to the parents whom a man is thankful for his life. Often we go back to the thought that without our parents we simply would have not been here. From here, it is a small step to think about the creating love of God!

However, it is not that God creates us and then we are independent of him. He has kept us in existence the way the sun has kept its light in existence. If a small child is totally dependent on his parents and he needs them to survive, then they are an image of God who keeps us in existence. They have to hold the child and carry him. Is not a mother with a child under her heart an image of the Creator, of whom it is stated: *For in him we live and move and have our being.*[104]? These are correlations which are strongly engraved on the emotions of a child. When he experiences his total dependence on his parents, he also learns a childlike dependence on God. When the children are cradled in the arms of their parents they will feel carried and secure in their lives.

Finally, we also need the help of God to develop and use our own strengths. If the parents teach their child speaking, eating and walking, the child learns the general notion that he also needs help in unfolding his own strengths and talents.

Let us take God's Providence: The children experience again and again that the parents watch and provide for them in advance, so they will not hesitate to entrust themselves to God's Providence later in life.

God is guiding us through his commandments and by manifesting His will.

---

[104] Acts 17,28

This is my commandment, that you love one another, as I have loved you.[105]

Parents educating and disciplining their children participate in the authority of God. This is the foundation and reason for the Fourth Commandment. In this way, too, they are an image and representation of God.

Beside this fundamental image of God, the parents also play a large part in forming the concept of God in the lives of their children. If a family were generous with people in need, it would be later easy to find again this virtue in the next generation. If the parents are understanding and considerate that a child cannot achieve everything at the same time, he can easily grasp the image of the mercy of God. If he can find in his parents forgiveness time and again, he will not find it difficult to believe in the unending mercy of God. If he experiences much appreciation and care from his parents, it will be later easily understandable for him that the love of God belongs to his children. The same can be said of all the qualities of God that are known to us: meekness, loyalty, authority, perseverance, humaneness[106], friendliness, justice, holiness, etc. What about the small surprises that give us an idea of God's courteous love? What about the clear required limits, about the lovingly granted permissions, about the promotion of personal talents and temperaments? Or about the hearty atmosphere in the family, about the clean, orderly, and elegant dwelling? So many chances to make our Father in heaven known to His children…

All this can and should serve to ensure that the children acquire their first idea of God, by means of the life lived by the parents. Later it will not be foreign to them to learn their catechism for they have many connecting points that can help them build up their life in faith. All the goodness as well as the negative traces of habitual faults that the parents carry all through the years leave a lasting impression on the children. The parents can control which traces they leave behind, but

---

[105] Jn 15,12
[106] Tit 3,4

not the fact that they cause permanent imprints. It is like a recording: It runs and cannot be stopped; the only question is which colors and pictures flow in.

The Parents as an image of Christ and the Church

The parents are an image and likeness of God but also a symbol of Christ and the Church. The graces of the sacrament of matrimony cause an ever-growing resemblance to the heavenly Bride and Groom. The mother will always resemble the Church and the father, an image of Our Lord Jesus Christ. If the parents so faithfully comply with the sacrament for many years, they turn themselves into an image of Christ and the Church. They do not need to "concoct," no need to "pretend," it simply grows by itself.

> *And he said: "This is the kingdom of God, as though a man should cast seed into the earth, then sleep and rise, night and day, and the seed should sprout and grow without his knowing it. For itself the earth bears the crop, first the blade, then the ear, then the full grain in the ear.*[107]

By the image the parents present, the children know Christ and the Church more and more, especially when they are still young. Only after many years especially after the First Communion will the children's own faith and prayer life be established. Before that, they live through the examples of the parents.

The children will learn how Christ and the Church live for each other from the respect, esteem and love the parents have for each other. The unity of actions and education gives the children the idea that Christ and the Church always care for the salvation of their beloved children. Besides the fact that it is the daily bread of the parents to pray together, this prayer speaks of the tasks that God has given them. Their Catholic spirit and sense of faith unite the family with Christ and the Church. The influence of the liturgical year on the family life strengthens this connection even more. Especially the attend-

---
[107] Mk 4,26f

ing of Mass together, the contact to the trunk and the origin of their marriage, has a deciding influence on the whole education of the children!

Above all, the children find in their parents the attitudes and virtues of Christ and the Church. That is shown once again in detail by the example of Confession. How deeply moving it is to repeatedly receive forgiveness from the hands of the Church in the sacrament of Penance.

Whose sins you shall forgive, they are forgiven them.[108]

The spirit of forgiveness should interest us above all: Everything is forgotten, everything is forgiven, what was red from sin, is now white as snow. The soul shines in the radiance of grace, Our Lord Jesus Christ has taken his sins away, the wounds of the soul are healed and he has made the large part of the reparation by himself. What an enormous gift! The sinner is spared and lifted up. The protection of sinners goes so far that from now on, the seal of confession is in force. Nothing, absolutely nothing can be spoken of by the priest. Should he violate the seal of confession, he will be excommunicated with an excommunication that only the Pope himself can unbind! The protection and the sparing of a sinner go that far!

The bruised reed he shall not break, and smoking flax he shall not quench.[109]

Of course, the parents must practice goodness and severity so that the children will be used to the observance of God's commandments. However, what if the child has violated it once again? Is not this the moment in which he should be guided to be sorry for his sins and where he should experience the protection that Christ and the Church have wanted for sinners? To some people it is perhaps a new idea; that is why it is once more emphasized: Should not the children learn something about forgiveness and mercy of God by the way parents forgive them? How about if in a family there was a rule that forgiven faults will never be mentioned again? How

---

[108] Jn 20,23
[109] Is 42,3

about if a child can go to his parents with the same trust as when we go to Confession? What would that mean for the spirit in the family! Herein also there lies a chance for the parents to spread goodness.

> **In any case, this example leads us to the idea that parents should take the sacrament of matrimony very seriously in educating their children. They are "consecrated" to the symbol for Christ and the Church. They should therefore keep that in mind, also in bringing up their children. A wide area is being opened here...!**

It is reasonable to point out a further consequence: The living of the sacrament means so much for the preparation of vocations. It would be a great injustice if the parents force or suggest to a child a vocation that he does not have. On the other hand, they have a preliminary duty in this matter. Because what does a young child need to hear the calling of God and follow it? He requires love for Our Lord Jesus Christ, for the Church and for souls. If a father is a loving father who through the years has resembled Jesus Christ, the mother has become resembling to the Church, and both are filled with love for immortal souls, how should a heart of a child not grow with the love needed for a vocation?

Nowadays, millions are spent for children to have a good Catholic education. The care for the future of the family, of Church and society presses us to make great sacrifices and rightly so. Is not this also an encouraging factor for the parents to do their part at home? Schools are an "artificial" means of education, but the life of the parents is the "most natural" way!

Finally, the sacrament of matrimony offers an excellent protection against the rampant errors of our age. We are living in an age of liberalism and secularism. Liberalism teaches independence from God, the Catholic Church, and revelation and promotes the total freedom from all binding duties. Secularism teaches the separation of the world from God, of society from religion, of family from the Church. Consequently, the spirit of independence from God has become more and more rampant and has led the world into a new "ice age."

And because iniquity will prevail, the charity of the many will grow cold.[110]

Many parents ask themselves anxiously how they can protect their family against this spirit of independence and the separation of life from religion. The answer lies in the sacrament of matrimony: If the father would really give the mother to drink the wine of Cana, that is, if he really loves her as Christ loves his Church, it will be not difficult for the mother to submit herself under the guidance of the father as the Church submits herself to Christ. The children have then a lovable and living example in their father and their mother; that authority is not tyranny and that submission and obedience are typically Christian.[111] With this, there lives a very different spirit in the family and in the hearts of the children, than in society today.

---

[110] Mt 24,12
[111] Phil 2,8

Downwards or Upwards?

The reader has now an idea in what framework the Catholic marriage stands, with what it is connected, what are their fruits. However, we still need to look at an important fact: Experience shows that people transform and change. It is the same with love. Love changes, there is no question; the real question is, in which direction is it going?

For the moment, let us take the fire as an example: In the initial phase, it crackles and blazes brightly. Soon after, it burns more calmly but also hotter because it more perfectly burns material from the environment. Finally, the flame subsides but there is far more glow that radiates widely, much more widely than the crackling fire at the beginning. Even from afar, one can put his hands out in the direction of the coals and feel the comforting warmth.

Fire has its different phases, which should not be opposed against each other. Likewise, the love in marriage has also different phases, each have their own entitlement and signification. The spouses will be older and more mature and so their love can also be more mature. Only one thing is not allowed to happen: That the love for each other decreases! It is also said of the love among spouses: *Love never ends.* [112] Only when death separates marriage and the spouses enter to the heavenly marriage feast the sacrament of matrimony also ends, no seconds before that! The spouses live until then as representatives of Christ and the Church and are responsible for the ways they live the sacrament of matrimony.

---

[112] 1 Cor 13,8

However, how does it happen that some marriages are more or less a friendly camaraderie and "fellowship" and the spouses only live side-by-side or like roommates? Nothing has happened and yet love has gone cold!

The reason for this downward direction lies often in the lack of the signs of love about which we have spoken about in the chapter "Signs of Love." These signs cannot be lacking "without very greatest damage for the marriage."

Instead of these signs, "shortcuts" and "simplifications" have established themselves: The spouses only speak about "useful topics," otherwise they are reserved and superficial in dealing with each other; one does not share his or her secrets and experiences anymore; they only talk about trivial things; with personal topics, they are cut short with each other. One no longer listens properly; he or she notices the marriage partner only just 30 percent. They take less and less time for each other. There are more and more calculations in the behavior. The words in the conversations sound matter-of-fact but chilly. The tone slowly becomes hard and sharp. One does not know what the word "love" could be used for anymore. They have known each other for so long and think that the other does not deserve it anymore. Criticisms are bluntly expressed because the situation seems clear. Finally, both have given up working on their relationship. It is "reduced," "straight forward," and "concluded."

Instead of arguing theoretically about it now, why things should change, we rather give our reader another example: What would you think of a priest who quickly prays his breviary in the morning, celebrates the Mass and then occupies himself with his favorite topics and hobbies for the rest of the day? If the faithful call, he does not answer the phone, or puts them off with general words so that he can quickly go back to his hobbies. He has adjusted to this idea that he is achieving nothing. The faithful have long ceased asking for his advice. He will take a fresh shirt and an old book for the sermon on Sunday, there is no defaulting in private prayer but it is minimal and impersonal, etc. Nothing great has happened, but nothing moves anymore either.

The reader probably has realized this marriage and this priesthood are comparable: The initial love is dormant; the engagement shortened, simplified, reduced and limited to the "essentials." Instead of action and commitment, the principle of simplification rules.

The causes could be: age, daily routine, disappointments, forgetfulness of the heart, or very simply and directly: Egotism, selfishness. All these possible causes have something in common: Nothing great has happened in detail. Like a chain that has many links, so are these hearts described above paralyzed with metal chains, chains that are only made up of small links. Through these "simplifications" and "shortcuts," the married couple has gone to the cellar, only to find out with surprise, where their marriage "has ended up." As a result, they live for themselves... but they don't *grow*. Children who are not growing put their parents in deepest concern. For it is understandable that life has always something to do with growth.

Instead of many arguments, we only want to cite the view of the Lord. The gospel speaks of a man who simply "went" to a wedding without preparing himself for the feast. His clothing was an everyday outfit. He did not make an effort to adjust himself to the royal wedding feast; he thought, *"This is enough as is!"*

> *Now the king went in to see the guests, and he saw there a man who had not on a wedding garment. And he said to him, "Friend, how didst thou come in here without a wedding garment?" But he was speechless. Then the king said to the attendants: "Bind his hands and feet and cast him forth into the darkness outside, where there will be the weeping, and the gnashing of teeth."*[113]

Because no married couple wants to live under such a curse, there is only one possibility: Turn back!

Instead of paralyzing the love through the lack of signs of love and ever greater simplifications, they should live again! Why not lay these injustices in the hands of Our Lord in a

---

[113] Mt 22,11ff

good confession? The first step is to turn to Mary! She will hurry to Jesus and say to him *They have no more wine.*[114] And then love will grow and increase again, instead of decreasing. If love grows again, it should go in the direction of "living" instead of the direction of "shortcut" and "reduction." That is when the expectation of Our Lord is fulfilled:

> *I have chosen you, and have appointed you that you should go and bear fruit -, and that your fruit should remain!*[115]

Then the Lord himself will be in the midst of the spouses and families again:

> *For where two or three are gathered together for my sake, there am I in the midst of them.*[116]

And now, dear spouses: Cheers!

---

[114] Joh 2,3
[115] Joh 15,16
[116] Mt 18,20

Text composed in Book Antiqua, 11 pt.
Titles in Luminari, 12 and 21 pt.

Laus Deo Virginique Matri
2015